MW00388832

# Synthetic and Exotic Scale Jazz Improvisation Etudes

## For Treble Clef Instruments

## Scott McGill

Copyright © 2014 Thomas Scott McGill

All Rights Reserved

ISBN-10: 978-1495494529

ISBM-13: 1495494527

To Meredith and Declan with Love

**Table of Contents:**

**Acknowledgements**

I wish to thank Tom Giacabetti who first introduced me to the scale materials contained within this text which inspired me to write these etudes. I also wish to thank Daniel Mullen, whose work on preparing the musical notation was vital to making this book possible.

# Foreword

This book focuses on the use of Synthetic and Exotic scales as melodic material over jazz type chord progressions. A variety of scale transpositions or tonics are utilized to illustrate some of the many options for scale use over a given chord or sequence of chords. Brackets are used to describe which scale transposition is at use at any given moment. The scales utilized in this text vary in construction and fall into one of the following categories:

- Common Scales from the Western Musical Tradition
- Scales from Non-Western Musical Traditions
- Scales which feature intervallic alteration of the above two categories
- Synthetic Scales

A few of these scales extend beyond the octave so no octave repetition will be present. In some instances, one scale is used to sound over two or more chords. All examples are in treble clef.

Each scale will be given before each etude (usually, but not always using the note C as a tonic) for ease of transposition so that the reader can quickly grasp the musical content of each melodic line and understand the intervallic relationship between the melodic line and the underlying harmony. This will also make it convenient for the instrumentalist to practice the scales in all keys and ranges of his or her instrument. Many of the scales do not have standardized names, so feel free to rename them if this is of benefit to you.

Guitarists, Bassists, Violinists etc. can play these examples and cales in all keys and octaves starting on all fingers and strings. Reed and Brass players can practice them in all keys throughout the range of their instruments using various articulations, and Keyboardists can practice them through the full range of their instrument hands separate, together, and with chordal accompaniment. Also, all scales can be rotated to produce modal inversions, formed into arpeggios that start on any scale degree, and harmonized to fully investigate the chordal possibilities that each one possesses.

The rhythmic content of each example varies, but generally stays within the jazz tradition. Tempo indications are not given so that the musician can apply and practice the lines according to his or her own taste, rhythmic preferences, and technical potential. When double or triple stops occur, simply choose the notes you wish to play according to your musical taste and your instrument's capability. These examples are not modeled after a particular artist or style. Any such similarities are unintentional and coincidental.

The notation style utilized is traditional. Once a note is altered with an accidental within a measure, it remains altered until the bar line is passed. Additional accidentals are used in different ranges for clarity. For example, if an F note on the top line of the staff is altered to F#, any F notes following in a different octave (for example an F in the first space of the staff) will be assumed to be unaltered unless an accidental is given. Although most of the examples do not utilize a key signature, a few do for optimum clarity in reading.

These etudes illustrate a relative few of the great many melodic applications of Synthetic and Exotic scales in relation to jazz harmonic patterns. I hope that this text helps to inspire new ideas and concepts for the creative musician.

Thomas Scott McGill
Hove, U.K.
February 7, 2014

# Lydian Dominant b9 Scale

# Leading Tone Major

# Enigmatic (Lydian b9, #5, b13)

# Lydian #2, #5

Scale

# Neapolitan Minor (Phrygian #7)

# Phrygian #11

# Dorian #5

## Dorian #5 (continued)

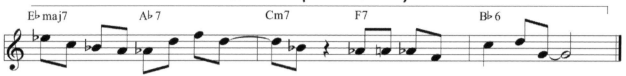

# Altered Pentatonic Scales

## Altered Pentatonic Scales (continued)

# Major Pentatonic

Scale

# Major Pentatonic (continued)

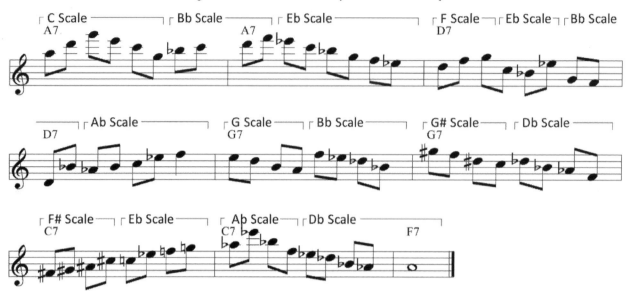

# Augmented 6th/Dominant 7th

# Augmented 6th

# Locrian Leading Tone

# Altered Minor Ninth

# Locrian Pentatonic

## Locrian Pentatonic (continued)

# bII7 Melodic Minor

Scale (for B7)

## bII7 Melodic Minor (continued)

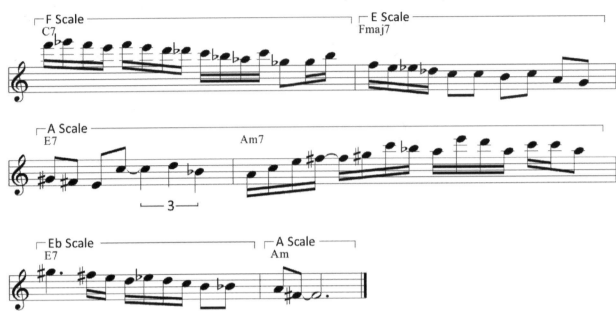

# Dorian b9

Scale

# Dorian #11

Scale

23

## Dorian #11 (continued)

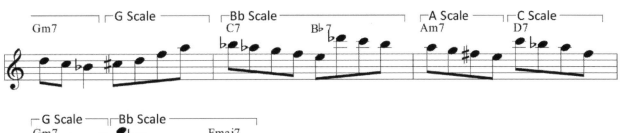

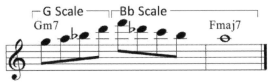

# Dorian b5

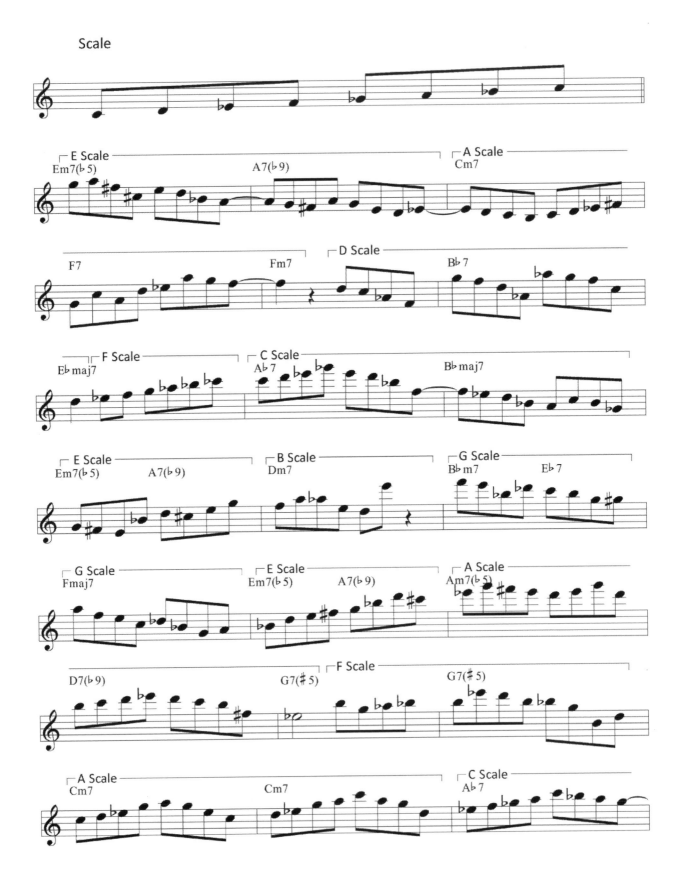

## Dorian b5 (continued)

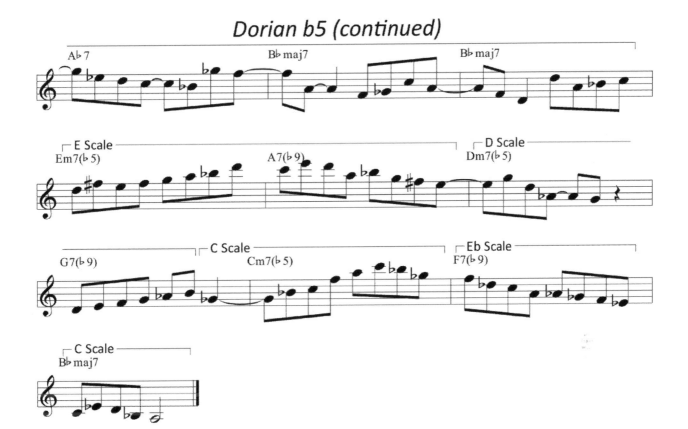

# b9, #5

Scale

# Dom 7 #9

# Neapolitan Lydian Hexatonic

Scale

## Neapolitan Lydian Hexatonic (continued)

# Major 7 b5

# Lydian Augmented

Scale

# Major

# Major 7 #9

# Lydian Bebop

# Persian

# Persian (continued)

# Altered Dominant b9 #11

# Oriental (Locrian Major 3rd)

## Oriental (Locrian Major 3rd) (continued)

# Augmented 13 #9

Scale

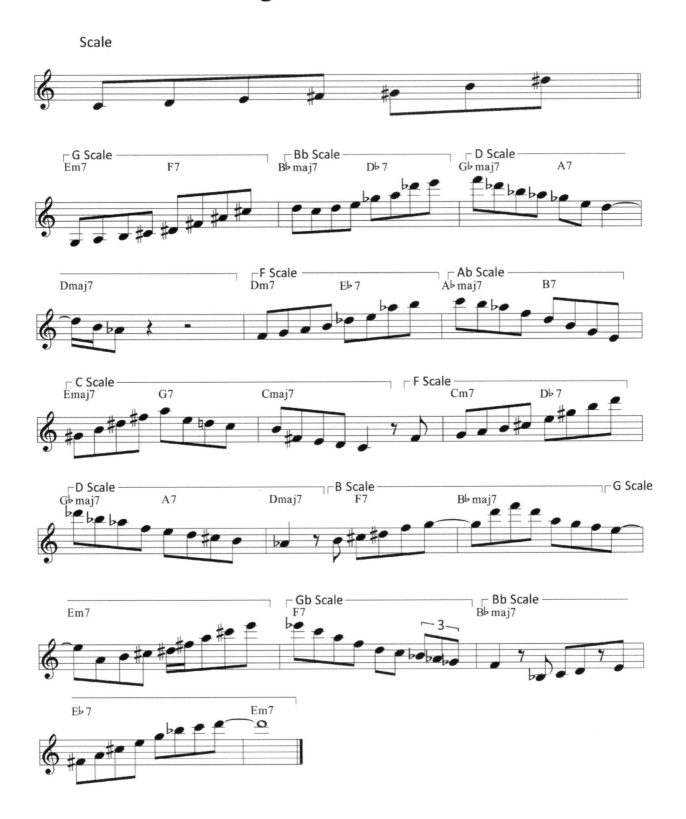

# Tonic Major 6th Dominant

Scale (for Ab7)

# Hungarian Major

Scale

# Harmonic Minor/Lydian (Hungarian Minor)

Scale

# Lydian b13

# 2nd mode Diminished (no #11)

Scale

# Diminished b9 (no #5)

# Diminished Perfect 4th

# Diminished Major 7

# Diminished b9

# Diminished b13

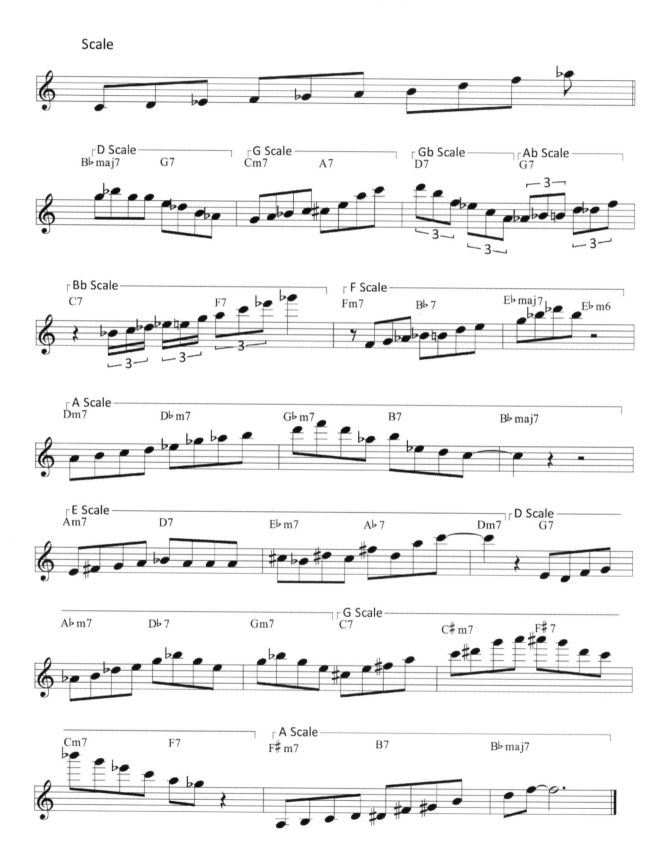

# Lydian Augmented b9

# C Augmented #4

Scale

# Lydian Augmented #6

# Lydian Augmented #9

# Augmented 13

# Augmented 9th

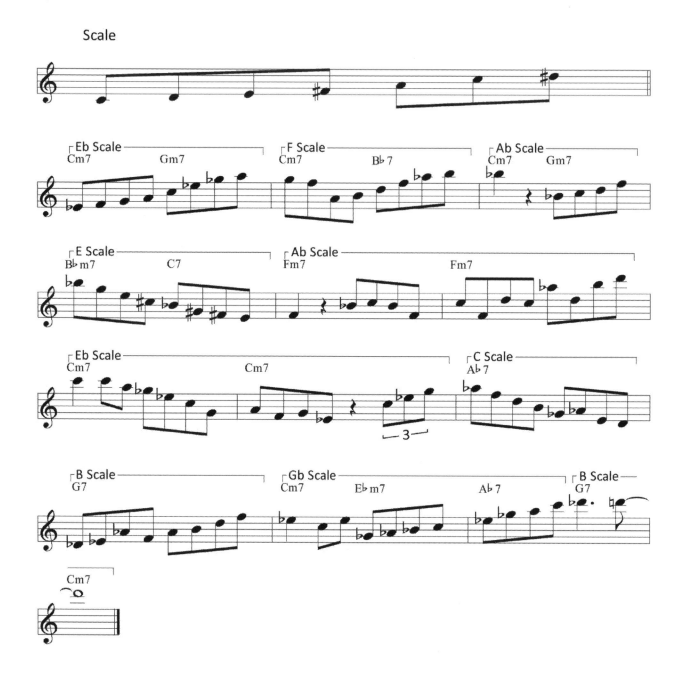

Made in the USA
Middletown, DE
24 October 2021

50931215R00040